# Introduction

Long-distance relationships (LDRs) are unique and challenging. Whether separated by a few hours or an entire ocean, work commitments or visa restrictions, being apart from the one you love can test your patience, resilience, and communication skills in ways you never could have imagined. And yet, for many couples, the distance doesn't weaken their bond—it can in fact make it unbreakable. When nurtured with care, an LDR can become a powerful testament to the depth of your connection and the love that transcends physical proximity.

This book is designed to offer guidance, support, and practical advice for anyone navigating a long-distance relationship. Whether you're just starting out or have been doing this for years, the unique dynamics of LDRs require a different approach to communication, trust, and emotional connection.

Over the following chapters, we'll explore the tools and strategies that can help make the distance feel more manageable. From staying emotionally connected and keeping the spark alive, to tackling challenges like communication barriers and conflicts, this guide aims to empower you to not just survive the distance but thrive in it.

We'll also address specific challenges like dealing with jealousy, planning reunions, and maintaining intimacy when physical presence isn't an option.

Whether you're in a relationship separated by geography, or even one that spans different cultures or time zones, this book will provide you with the insights and resources you need to keep your relationship strong.

Ultimately, an LDR is not about enduring the distance; it's about cherishing the connection that keeps you together regardless of it.

Let this book be your companion as you navigate the ups and downs of long-distance love and remember that the distance between you and your partner doesn't define your relationship—your love does.

# Chapter 1: Am I Compatible with a Long-Distance Relationship?

Long-distance relationships (LDRs) are not for everyone, and it's important to start by asking yourself if you're truly compatible with the unique challenges they bring, and make no mistake, there are many.

Long-distance relationships can be emotionally draining, and at times, you will find yourself feeling alone in moments when you need support the most. The lack of physical intimacy often causes many LDRs to fail. You'll also find that, in addition to the emotional challenges, there are ever-present practicality and financial difficulties. Maintaining two separate lives, two households, and possibly even paying for frequent travel, can become a significant burden.

But what does compatibility with a long-distance relationship look like?

There are certain qualities and mindsets that can help partners thrive despite the distance. We will cover each in this chapter briefly, however, all will be covered in much more detail throughout the book.

## Trust

Trust is a non-negotiable in LDRs, if it is not there, your relationship will be a constant form of emotional trauma and unbearable torture. The distance means you can't be present in your partner's daily life, and this can lead to insecurity, jealousy and ultimately, conflict, if trust isn't firmly established. Your partner will have experiences, friends, and activities that you aren't part of, and that's something you need to learn to be okay with. Trust means allowing each other to live these lives without feeling the need to constantly check in and be informed of every movement. It means giving space for independence and recognizing that your partner's plans and time are just as valid as your own and that sometimes, you will be the last to know, but not jumping to conclusions because of that. Trust ultimately is a security blanket which allows you to sleep peacefully knowing your love is limitless and unbreakable, regardless of the situation. If trust has previously been an issue in previous relationships, it is important for you to really ask yourself honestly whether you can cope with the inevitable moments of disconnect and distance without suffering. Of course, trust is something that differs in different dynamics, so you need to really know that you can, will and want to trust your partner in even the hardest moments to always be truthful with you. It's okay to ask your partner to do small things to help build the foundations of trust, but not if that becomes a burden and intrusive in their life.

## Emotional Maturity

LDRs are not for those who are not self-aware; emotional maturity is essential. There will be times when distance creates a void and your connection feels strained. You may feel lonely, and it's important not to project those feelings of loneliness, frustration, or insecurity onto your partner and make those feelings their responsibility to fix. There will be days or even weeks where a comfortable level of contact isn't viable due to work, time zones, family or other life commitments. Learning to cope with those moments and still find fulfillment outside of your relationship is crucial. You need to be able to communicate these feelings effectively without turning them into accusations or resentment and most importantly, self-manage those feelings and self-sooth.

## Compatible Communication Styles

Whether you have compatible communication styles is something you should consider. If one of you is uncomfortable on video calls and prefers to text, whilst the other is the exact opposite you need to be realistic about whether that is manageable. Being compatible doesn't necessarily mean the same, it means you are both able and willing to understand and accept your own communication styles and meet in the middle. It is helpful if you're able to identify your own needs and are self-aware enough to be flexible about how those needs are met. If you are unable to work around your partners preferred communication styles, your relationship may often feel difficult and strained.

## Support

While not essential, having a supportive social circle and family can make a significant difference in how you cope with the distance. It's important not to rely solely on your partner for emotional support. Surrounding yourself with understanding and compassionate friends and family can help fill the emotional gaps that LDRs often create. Having loved ones you can turn to when you're struggling will make you feel more resilient. It also ensures you don't miss out on experiences and social activities typically associated with relationships. With a strong support network, you'll have people ready to spend time with and create memories, while keeping your partner close in spirit on your adventures.

## Patience and Acceptance

Finally, you must accept that it won't look the same as a traditional relationship. You may not have a plus-one for every event or get to share everyday experiences. The reality is that there will be sacrifices, but if both partners are committed and possess the right qualities, these challenges can be overcome. The goal is not to mirror what other relationships look like, but to create a fulfilling partnership despite the physical distance.

The other consideration is that the aim of an LDR is not always to 'close the distance' as quickly as possible and feeling that way will bring pressure and stress to your relationship. You need to look within yourself to see if you can manage the patience, uncertainty and flexibility your LDR will require.

As you consider a long-distance relationship, reflect on whether these qualities resonate with you and your partner. Understanding these dynamics is the first step in creating a strong foundation for your relationship, no matter the miles between you.

# Chapter 2: Safety Concerns Presented in Long-Distance Relationships

The distance in LDRs can sometimes bring out the worst in us, especially in relationships where partners haven't met face-to-face. As such, those in long distance relationships can tend to be more tolerant of big emotions and difficulty adjusting, which is understandable and absolutely justified, however, that additional tolerance can leave people open to being scammed or finding themselves trapped in an abusive relationship. LDR partners are more readily accepting of emotional difficulty, making them more vulnerable, and without body language and normal social situations, bad intentions can be hidden much more easily.

Whilst this isn't a nice part of LDRs to think about, it is an essential one, particularly when you meet your partner online. Being aware of potential red flags both in yourself and partner can help you avoid falling into toxic patterns, whilst also being vigilant and seeing the difference between poor emotional control, struggling with the challenges of your LDR Vs. someone attempting to scam you or a potentially abusive partner.

All that said, try not to jump to conclusions about

your partner being a bad person after one conflict or one example of poor coping strategies, but likewise, don't make excuses for them long-term if they are unwilling to recognize and work on themselves. It is very important that you recognize any potential red flags in your relationship and be realistic about where they may come from.

**Controlling Behaviour**

For example, controlling behavior is a common issue in LDRs and often stems from insecurity or trust issues. If your partner insists on having constant access to your location or demands frequent updates on your whereabouts, this could be a red flag. While occasionally sharing locations can be helpful—like when you're on a long trip or in an unsafe situation—it should never feel like an obligation. Healthy location sharing is voluntary and mutually agreed upon, not pressured. If your partner consistently uses your location to monitor you or guilt-trip you about your plans, it's time to reassess whether that behavior is healthy.

If you feel uncomfortable, don't hesitate to confide in a trusted friend, family member, or professional to seek advice on handling the situation. It's critical that neither partner feels pressured into location sharing or giving more detail about their everyday than they are comfortable with. If your partner insists on sharing locations despite your discomfort, this could indicate a toxic dynamic.

Unfortunately, the rise of anonymous online advice

groups and pages can mislead people into toxic behaviors unwittingly. Often, people asking questions about location sharing get a good proportion of responses which advise the "OP" (Original Poster) that anyone who will not share their location has something to hide. This is a hard mindset to argue with, but it is one you should avoid falling into, we all have a right to privacy and alone time. Of course, these sites and groups rarely have replies coming from people with any kind of accolade or qualification and therefore a culture has been created where the blind lead the blind simply by belonging to a majority opinion in a very small corner of our green earth.

Other manifestations of control can creep in subtly, but in a long-distance relationship (LDR), where trust and independence are crucial, controlling behaviors can be especially damaging. Control may start off as seemingly innocent requests but can quickly escalate. For example, if your partner may start trying to dictate what you wear, telling you certain outfits are inappropriate or making you feel uncomfortable about your choices, this is a sign of unhealthy control. They may also attempt to limit your activities by insisting on knowing what you're always doing, questioning your plans, or making you feel guilty for spending time with friends or family. In extreme cases, they might even tell you outright who you can and cannot see, isolating you from your support network under the guise of protecting the relationship. Even if these "requests" from your partner are because of their own religion and culture, you do not have to comply, it is up to you whether you will embrace their lifestyle and if they require that from you, it needs to be mutually agreed, not dictated.

It is generally an escalating behavior, starting subtly but gradually becoming more forceful and hurtful. If you notice that your partner is increasingly forcing you into complying with their decisions about your life—what you should do, where you should go, or who you should talk to—it's important to talk to them about setting healthy boundaries and setting out how their behavior is making you feel. If your partner is unable to reflect and improve, you should consider leaving the relationship. Both partners should always feel free to live their lives without excessive interference. Two people in a relationship should bring joy and support to each other's day, not control and misery.

When someone tries to control aspects of your day-to-day life, it can lead to feelings of resentment, isolation, and emotional dependency, all of which can be toxic in any relationship, but especially in an LDR where trust is already tested by distance.

### Financial Abuse

Another red flag is financial abuse. If your partner starts telling you how to spend your money or guilt-trips you into sending money to them, be cautious. While offering your partner financial support may develop naturally in long-term committed relationships, you should never feel pressured or obligated to give more than you're comfortable with. Many scammers online expertly manipulate emotions to make it seem like helping them financially was your idea. To avoid falling into this trap, if you do choose to help, consider sending practical help—such as groceries or supplies delivered directly to them—instead of money. This can verify the legitimacy of their requests.

### Emotional Manipulation

Emotional manipulation, such as gaslighting or minimizing your feelings, is another risk in LDRs. If your partner frequently tells you that you're "too sensitive" or "paranoid," this could be a form of gaslighting, making you doubt your own emotions and memories. Healthy relationships address concerns through open communication, not by dismissing or twisting the truth. If you find yourself feeling confused or anxious after conversations, reach out to a trusted person for perspective. Misunderstandings can happen, especially with language or cultural differences, but if your partner frequently denies your reality, it's time to reconsider the relationship.

### Refusal to Commit

Another harmful behavior to watch out for is avoiding commitment or exclusivity. If your partner is hesitant to define the relationship or dodges conversations about commitment, this could be a sign they aren't fully invested or have another relationship or even family already and are using you for the emotional connection and confidence boost or for financial help. While relationships take time to develop, especially at a distance, there should be clarity about where things are heading and what you both want with agreeable timeframes if you both are serious about making it work. You'll not always agree, but there needs to be respect, understanding and compromise otherwise you may have reason to be suspicious.

By recognizing these red flags early on, you can set boundaries and protect yourself from toxic behaviors that could cause you emotional and financial harm. Every relationship has its challenges, but a long-distance relationship should never feel like an emotional or psychological burden.

### Online Scams

Another risk unique to LDRs, especially those initiated online, is the possibility of scams. Sadly, some people enter relationships not for love but for personal gain—whether financial or otherwise. One significant scam involves someone feigning love to gain immigration status or a visa. Scammers often use emotional manipulation to build trust, rushing into the relationship with grand declarations of love and discussing marriage or visas prematurely. They may avoid direct questions about their personal life or seem vague about important details.

It's essential to verify your partner's identity and intentions early in the relationship. This includes video calls, background research, and paying attention to any inconsistencies in their story. In the UK, tools like Claire's Law allow you to check for a history of abuse, and other countries have similar systems. Always trust your instincts—if something feels off, it probably is. It's also a good idea to Google your partners name and location to see if anything concerning comes up, such as news articles or public records that might reveal a hidden criminal history. Trust your instincts—if something feels off or too rushed, take a step back and reassess the situation. It's better to be cautious and protect yourself than to ignore red flags that could have serious consequences down the line. Being vigilant, communicating openly, and taking the time to get to know your partner's background will help safeguard you against the risks of being scammed or manipulated.

Remember, scammers are happy to play the "long-game" even if that means feigning a relationship over the course of years, if it means they get what they want out of it. Don't use time as a test.

### Love Bombing

Love bombing is a common manipulation tactic in

unhealthy relationships and is also often used by scammers. It occurs when someone overwhelms you with excessive attention, affection, and praise very quickly—often in the early stages of a relationship. While it might seem romantic, this tactic is used to create emotional dependence. Once you're hooked, they may become controlling, possessive, or abusive.

If you feel overwhelmed by the intensity or rushed by the relationship's pace, take a step back and talk to someone outside the relationship. Healthy relationships allow space for reflection and boundaries; anyone who discourages you from sharing details with others or tries to isolate you is a red flag.

## What to Do If You're Concerned About Abuse

If you start to feel like your LDR is becoming abusive—whether emotionally, psychologically, or even financially—it's important to acknowledge those feelings and act. Abuse in long-distance relationships can be subtle at first, often taking the form of manipulation, gaslighting, or emotional blackmail. Your partner might guilt you into feeling responsible for their emotional well-being, demand constant attention, or punish you with silent treatment if you don't meet their needs.

If you suspect you're in an abusive relationship, start by talking to someone you trust—whether a friend, family member, or therapist—so you don't feel isolated. Keep records of conversations and interactions that make you feel uncomfortable or unsafe, as this documentation may be important later. If you feel unsafe or pressured, set clear boundaries with your partner, and don't hesitate to cut off communication if those boundaries aren't respected.

In cases where you fear your partner's identity might be false, or you're concerned about the authenticity of your relationship, it's crucial to be proactive. Use online resources to verify their identity—look them up on social media, do a reverse image search on their photos, and try to confirm details about their life independently. If your partner refuses to video chat or provide proof of who they are after months of communication, this is a serious red flag.

Additionally, if you're concerned about your safety or want to know more about your partner's past, tools like Claire's Law (in the UK) or similar laws in other countries can help you request information from authorities about any history of abuse. Many countries also have public records available online, so make sure to check for any criminal records or warning signs.

Trust your intuition—if something feels off, it probably is. You deserve to feel safe and respected in your relationship, and taking steps to protect yourself is always a priority. Never feel guilty for prioritizing your well-being over a relationship, especially if it's becoming unhealthy or dangerous.

If you do suspect you have been scammed or are concerned about your safety due to threats or abusive behaviors, speak to your local police force as soon as you are able, using the non-emergency number for most situations, and the emergency number if you feel you are in immediate danger.

# Chapter 3: Learning to Trust

Trust really is the cornerstone of any healthy relationship, but even the most trusting individuals can find themselves struggling in a long-distance relationship. When you're not physically present with your partner, there's often a greater sense of vulnerability, and it can be challenging to maintain the same level of security you might feel in a relationship where you see each other regularly. The distance leaves more room for uncertainty, and it can amplify insecurities that you never knew you had.

In this chapter, we'll explore why even trusting people may struggle in LDRs, the challenges you'll need to overcome, and healthy ways to build and maintain trust. We'll also highlight some toxic habits to avoid and how to be mindful of your own behavior to prevent self-sabotage.

## Why Trust is Harder in Long-Distance Relationships

Even in the most secure long-distance relationships, trust can be hard to nurture, and trust is something which needs constant care to remain. You don't have the daily physical presence that often provides reassurance, and instead, rely on digital communication. This distance can increase feelings of vulnerability and make you question things more easily than you might in a face-to-face relationship. You may find yourself wondering whether your partner is being honest about their activities or their feelings, which is a natural challenge.

To navigate these difficulties, it's essential to recognize that a certain amount of insecurity and uncertainty is normal in LDRs. Embrace it as a reflection of how much you love and care for your partner. Understanding that your worries are natural can help you address them constructively and keep them in proportion.

Several factors make trusting more difficult in LDRs, such as:

- **Limited communication:** While technology makes it easier to stay connected, miscommunications or lack of contact on busy days can cause anxiety.
- **Inability to see your partner's actions:** When you're apart, you can't observe how your partner behaves in social settings or how they handle stress in real life. This can lead to mistakenly interpreting their bad days as problems with you.
- **Increased independence:** Each partner is living a separate life, with friends, work, and social activities that don't involve the other. This can sometimes lead to feelings of jealousy or fear of being replaced.

- **Loneliness:** In times of need, you might crave your partner's support, but distance makes it harder for them to be there in a meaningful way. This can erode trust over time, replacing it with feelings of betrayal and resentment.

To build and maintain trust in an LDR, it's important to recognize the feelings and habits that can compromise it. Self-awareness allows reflection and growth.

Jealousy

Jealousy is one of the biggest challenges in an LDR. When your partner spends time with friends or attends events without you, it's natural to feel insecure or left out. This is where effective communication becomes vital. Rather than imposing restrictions on your partner's activities, it's better to express your feelings openly when you feel like you need more from them. Often, simple changes, like occasional check-ins or giving you a heads-up about their plans, can ease your concerns. However, it's crucial to work on your insecurities without controlling your partner's actions. Stop and question why you feel the way you do and decide whether it's caused by logic or by the passion and love of missing your partner.

Overthinking

LDRs provide a lot of alone time, which can

quickly lead to overthinking. You may start reading too much into every message, delay, or change in routine. If your partner doesn't respond to a text right away or seems distant during a call, it's easy to jump to conclusions, thinking they might be losing interest or distracted by something forbidden. Instead, break down the need you currently have that hasn't been met, and figure out how you can overcome those feelings with logic and resilience. Using a journal or an anxiety workbook can help work through these worries. You can also set aside time to talk with your partner and ask for support, which might lead to something as simple as planning a digital date night or scheduling a more thorough catch-up.

## Insecurities

LDRs can magnify any pre-existing insecurities, and you may even find new ones you never imagined you would have. You may worry that your partner is finding someone else, that they're not as invested, or that the relationship isn't progressing as it should. These insecurities, if left unchecked, can cause you to lash out, make unfair accusations or cause the relationship to end. As with overthinking, you must be able to be self-reflective and consider why you feel the way you do and work on yourself rather than push your emotions onto your partner expecting them to save the day at their own emotional expense. It is reasonable to ask your partner to consider and be aware of your feelings and emotional needs, but not if you are expecting them to change their life and neglect their own needs to better suit yours.

## Overcoming Trust Issues

The key to building trust in an LDR is consistent and transparent communication. Regular check-ins and open discussions about your feelings can help ease the natural anxieties that arise from distance. It's essential to be honest about your struggles and vulnerable enough to share your concerns before they escalate into bigger issues. If both partners can approach trust with honesty and patience, it becomes much easier to overcome doubts.

### Setting Boundaries and Expectations

As cultural differences can often be a problem, establishing clear boundaries and expectations is key to maintaining trust. This includes discussing how often you'll communicate, what things you expect your partner to tell you about in advance or within a quick timeframe, along with what you're comfortable with when it comes to socializing separately, and how you both plan to manage your independence while staying committed. Knowing what each of you expects from the relationship can prevent misunderstandings and hurt feelings.

### Trust the Process

Remember, building trust is a process that takes time, and you'll need to be patient with yourselves and each other. Remind yourself that trust isn't built overnight, but through consistency, reliability and presence. It is so much harder in a long-distance relationship, but where there is love, commitment, respect and a desire to make it work, it will come. Remember "innocent until proven guilty" and don't allow yourself to be emotionally led, instead leading with time to process and then appropriate and respectful questions where you still have doubts or concerns.

### Focus on Quality Time

Even though you can't be physically together, make sure you make time for meaningful communication and connection to stop doubt and insecurities creeping in. Rather than just chatting for the sake of it, plan quality conversations where you check in with each other on an emotional level. This could be through video calls, deep conversations about life, or even sending thoughtful messages to each other throughout the day.

## Toxic Habits to Avoid

When navigating trust in a long-distance

relationship, it's crucial to be aware of your own behaviors. Certain habits can be destructive and undermine the trust you're working hard to build.

### Constant Monitoring

One toxic behavior to avoid is the need to constantly check on your partner. This might include frequently asking for updates on where they are, who they're with, or what they're doing. While some level of curiosity is natural, obsessive monitoring signals a lack of trust and can create tension in the relationship. It can also cause anxiety and mental health problems for you both.

### Demanding Proof

Asking your partner for proof of their whereabouts or activities, such as sharing their location or sending photos or screenshots, is controlling and abusive behavior. Trust should be freely given, not forced. If you feel the need for constant proof, it's a sign that you are allowing your emotions to control you. Remember, there are few things that cannot be edited to look a certain way with photo editing apps, so if you don't trust your partners word, proof won't and should not be used to help.

## Emotional Manipulation and Guilt-Tripping

Be mindful of not using emotional manipulation to

control your partner's behavior. Emotional manipulation can be subtle, but it's harmful and can erode trust over time. In a long-distance relationship, where communication is often limited to texts, calls, and video chats, emotional manipulation can sometimes go unnoticed or be harder to recognize, making it essential to stay alert to these dynamics.

Guilt-tripping is a common form of emotional manipulation where one partner makes the other feel responsible for their emotional state or happiness. This can take many forms, such as the subcategories listed below.

**Blaming Your Partner for Your Emotions**

Phrases like "If you really loved me, you'd do this for me," or "You're making me feel so lonely by not calling more often" can place undue pressure on your partner and make them feel responsible for your emotional well-being. In an LDR, physical distance can amplify feelings of insecurity or loneliness, but it's crucial to communicate those emotions in a healthy way without making your partner feel guilty for not meeting all your emotional needs.

**Using Past Mistakes as Leverage**

Bringing up past arguments or mistakes to gain the upper hand in a current conversation can lead to a toxic cycle. This is particularly damaging in an LDR, where misunderstandings are common due to limited face-to-face interaction. If you feel hurt by something in the past, it's important to address it directly rather than use it as future leverage in unrelated situations.

## Emotional Dependency

In an LDR, it's natural to miss your partner and wish they were closer, but constantly placing the responsibility on them to "fix" your loneliness or emotional struggles can create an unhealthy dynamic. Statements like, "I wouldn't feel this way if you were available to talk more" or "I'm so unhappy because we're apart" can lead your partner to feel trapped and pressured to solve something that may not have an immediate solution.

## What to Do if Trust Is Broken

If trust is broken, whether through infidelity, dishonesty, or unmet expectations, it's important to take time to assess the situation. Trust can be rebuilt, but it requires effort from both partners. Open communication, sincere apologies, and a plan for moving forward are necessary to repair the damage.

It is very important you do have an unrushed conversation after the dust has settled so you understand how and why the trust was broken and how your partner feels about their actions, this gives you the opportunity to assess whether they feel remorse and ultimately, whether they are likely to repeat their actions.

If you find that trust continues to erode despite your best efforts, it's important to reflect on whether the relationship is still healthy and fulfilling for both of you. It's okay to step back and prioritize your emotional well-being if the relationship is causing more pain than joy, whether that is temporarily or permanently.

Learning to trust in a long-distance relationship is a journey that requires patience, communication, and self-awareness. It's normal to experience doubts, but by focusing on open communication, setting healthy boundaries, and being aware of toxic habits, you can cultivate a relationship built on mutual respect and trust. Remember, both partners must actively work toward maintaining that trust—because without it, the foundation of any relationship, especially one with distance, becomes shaky.

# Chapter 4: Understanding and Embracing Differences

One of the most powerful tools for maintaining a healthy long-distance relationship (LDR) is developing a deeper understanding of each other. Unlike couples who can rely on physical proximity to smooth over misunderstandings, long-distance couples benefit greatly from understanding their partner's personality, attachment style, and love language because they need to have this deeper understanding to navigate the distance. If you are wondering what the heck those things are, don't worry – we're about to dive into a beginner's guide. These insights should help you navigate potential friction points with empathy, understanding and ease. All the suggested resources are linked at the back of the book for you within the Useful Resources chapter.

Let's dive into looking at some of the ways you can learn more about each other using an array of online resources.

### 16 Personalities

A helpful tool for understanding your partner is the 16 Personalities test, which is based on the Myers-Briggs Type Indicator (MBTI). It's available for free online and categorizes people into 16 different personality types, focusing on traits like introversion vs. extroversion, thinking vs. feeling, and judging vs. perceiving. For example, one partner might be more introverted and need time alone to recharge, while the other is extroverted and thrives on social interaction.

Taking the test together can be a fun digital date, but more importantly, sharing your results helps you understand how your partner approaches the world. This understanding helps you find common ground and anticipate areas of potential conflict. For instance, if one partner is a Judging type (J) who prefers structure, and the other is a Perceiving type (P) who is more spontaneous, you can approach decisions—like planning visits or coordinating schedules—with greater awareness and flexibility. There is a great amount of detail available so you can really get into what each trait means and how it affects your relationship. There is a good reason they say knowledge is power, and this kind of information can even help in preventing escalation within conflict.

### Love Languages

Exploring love languages can also be beneficial, and you can find free tests on websites like LoveSpeak. Love languages refer to how we express and perceive love, with the five primary types being Words of Affirmation, Acts of Service, Receiving Gifts, Quality Time, and Physical Touch. In an LDR, knowing your partner's love language can help bridge the gap of physical separation. For example, if your partner values Words of Affirmation, regular, thoughtful texts or voice messages will go a long way in maintaining connection. Alternatively, if their love language is Acts of Service, finding ways to help them with tasks remotely can demonstrate care and effort, even from afar. Knowing what actions your partner is most likely to respond to when they're feeling down or insecure will quickly become your superpower.

**Attachment Styles**

Attachment styles, rooted in Attachment Theory, are another important aspect to understand. People generally have one of four attachment styles: Secure, Anxious, Avoidant, or Disorganized. For example, an Anxious partner may need frequent communication and reassurance in an LDR, while an Avoidant partner might prefer more space. Recognizing these patterns allows you to better support each other's needs without causing undue stress or misunderstanding.

Numerous free quizzes and resources online can help you identify your attachment styles, providing a better understanding of how each of you approaches relationships. This knowledge can help both partners feel more secure, supported, and prioritized in the relationship.

By taking the time to learn these aspects of each other's personalities, you build a more complete picture of how to nurture and support each other despite the distance. When conflicts do arise, as they inevitably will, you'll have a better framework for understanding why you and your partner might be reacting in certain ways. It allows you to communicate with empathy, rather than frustration.

### Neurodivergence

Many individuals fall on the wide spectrum of neurodivergence, which can influence how they communicate and experience relationships. Neurodivergence refers to differences in how people process information and think, including conditions like ADHD (Attention Deficit Hyperactivity Disorder) and Autism Spectrum Disorder (ASD). While these traits vary, it's important to recognize how they may affect communication and behavior in an LDR.

## ADHD

For someone with ADHD, focusing during long-distance conversations, such as video calls or text messages, might be challenging. They may forget to respond, lose track of time, or struggle with following through on plans. While these behaviors aren't intentional, they can cause frustration or feelings of neglect in their partner. Recognizing these tendencies can help reduce misunderstandings. Setting reminders or having scheduled communication times can create structure, making it easier for the ADHD partner to stay engaged. Instead of fixating on what your partner may struggle with, focus on the ways they show up for you in the relationship.

## Autism

In contrast, someone on the autism spectrum may face challenges with understanding non-verbal cues, tone, or emotional nuances—particularly in text messaging. They might struggle with sarcasm or miss subtle shifts in tone, leading to unintentional misunderstandings. Individuals with ASD often appreciate direct, clear communication, so it's helpful to be upfront about your emotions and needs, rather than expecting them to "read between the lines."

Moreover, people with ASD may prefer routines and predictability, so unexpected changes in communication—such as a missed call or a delayed response—can be more distressing for them than for a neurotypical partner. Being mindful of these preferences and accommodating them through shared expectations can help foster a stronger connection. Understanding and accommodating these neurodivergent traits requires patience and adaptability. Clear, direct communication and setting shared expectations can go a long way in easing these challenges.

By understanding your partner's personality, attachment style, love language, and neurodivergent traits (if applicable), you can build a more empathetic and resilient relationship. Embracing these differences not only strengthens your bond but also helps avoid unnecessary conflicts. Clear communication, mutual support, and an openness to learning about each other's unique needs are essential ingredients for a strong, healthy relationship—no matter the distance.

# Chapter 5: Self-Awareness and Emotional Maturity

Being in a long-distance relationship (LDR) is not just a test of love but also a profound journey in understanding oneself. A key foundation of a successful and content LDR, or any relationship, is emotional maturity. But what exactly is emotional maturity, and how does self-awareness play a role in building a stronger connection with your partner?

### What is Emotional Maturity?

Emotional maturity is the ability to navigate your feelings and reactions with grace, understanding, and self-awareness. It involves recognizing your emotions without being controlled by them, effectively communicating your needs, and managing conflict in a way that fosters growth rather than division. In an LDR, emotional maturity is crucial because physical distance can amplify feelings of insecurity, frustration, or loneliness, making it even more important to manage these emotions constructively.

A crucial aspect of emotional maturity is recognizing that your emotions are your responsibility. While your partner can support and validate you, they are not responsible for how you feel. In moments of difficulty, emotional maturity allows you to reflect on your reactions and see whether they're influenced by insecurity, past experiences, or external stress. It's also about pausing before reacting and choosing how to respond to challenges instead of lashing out. Emotional maturity involves realistic expectations—your partner won't always be able to meet your needs exactly as you'd prefer, and that's okay. Sometimes, external factors like work commitments or stress can affect their availability, or certain expressions of love may feel uncomfortable for them.

Rather than becoming frustrated or feeling unloved, emotional maturity means accepting that your partner may not always deliver in the way you desire and embracing their unique way of expressing love.

### Meeting in the Middle

If your partner's way of loving or communicating doesn't always align with your needs, the healthiest approach is to seek balance rather than perfection. Relationships thrive on mutual effort and understanding, not on one person conforming entirely to the other's needs.

For example, if one partner craves verbal reassurance and the other struggles with expressing emotions verbally, you might agree to find a compromise which enables reassurance to be offered in a way that feels comfortable for both. This might involve using written communication like thoughtful messages or setting aside dedicated time for emotional check-ins, rather than forcing daily emotional conversations that feel overwhelming for one partner.

Finding that middle ground is an act of love in itself, it shows that both of you are invested in the relationship and willing to adapt for the sake of your connection.

### Be Responsible for Your Own Growth

It is crucial to your own emotional growth to recognize that relationships often bring out our own flaws and worst habits. Sometimes, your interactions with your partner may highlight insecurities or emotional struggles that you didn't realize you had. For instance, you may discover that you're more anxious or controlling in certain situations, or that you struggle with vulnerability.

It's perfectly natural for your partner to want to help and support you when you're going through these emotional challenges, but it's important not to expect them to carry the full weight of your growth. Your partner can encourage and validate you, but they shouldn't feel like your therapist or responsible for fixing your inner struggles. Relying too heavily on them to "heal" you can put undue pressure on the relationship and ultimately lead to frustration for both partners.

Instead, emotional maturity involves recognizing when the relationship is highlighting issues in yourself and being proactive about working on them independently. This could mean seeking therapy, practicing mindfulness, or exploring personal development tools that help you manage your emotions in a healthier way. Your partner's support can complement this work, but the primary responsibility for your emotional well-being is yours.

## Self-Awareness in Relationships

Self-awareness is a key element of emotional maturity, especially in the context of a long-distance relationship. It means understanding your emotional triggers, insecurities, and habits and taking responsibility for them. It also means being able to step back and assess how your actions and behaviors are affecting the relationship.

When you're self-aware, you can recognize moments when your own emotional baggage is creating tension, and you can work to address it before it becomes a bigger issue. This might involve reflecting on why you're feeling jealous or insecure, rather than immediately blaming your partner. It also means being honest with yourself about your own needs and boundaries and communicating them clearly without expecting your partner to guess or read your mind.

It's important to approach self-awareness with a positive mindset. If you recognize you've been projecting your insecurities onto your partner, don't punish yourself. The key is to own it and find practical, positive ways to move forward.

**Overcoming Barriers to Success**

At the core of a successful long-distance relationship is the understanding that both partners are responsible for their own emotional well-being. Emotional maturity means knowing when to ask for support and when to take ownership of your growth. It's about communicating your needs clearly, but also accepting that your partner may not always be able to meet them exactly as you'd like.

By embracing differences in attachment styles, love languages, and emotional needs, and by finding ways to compromise and meet in the middle, you can build a stronger, more resilient connection with your partner. Ultimately, self-awareness and emotional maturity are about recognizing that relationships are not about perfection, but about growth—both individually and together.

# Chapter 6: Connecting with Your Partner and Getting to Know Them on a Deeper Level

Long-distance relationships often come with the challenge of maintaining a strong emotional connection without the benefit of physical presence. While physical closeness may be limited, emotional intimacy can be deepened through intentional communication and shared experiences. In this chapter, we'll explore creative ways to build a deeper bond with your partner, using both structured activities and spontaneous moments of connection to bridge the gap in your relationship.

One of our favorite resources is a book we found on Amazon called **Close the Distance by Hannah Smart**. This fantastic resource provides 52 weekly tasks designed to help couples tackle all aspects of their relationship, spanning over 8 categories to keep you connected, in love, laughing and sharing your day to day. These activities are designed to be completed together, giving you and your partner opportunities to engage in meaningful reflection and growth. By consistently investing time into these structured exercises, you can deepen your emotional bond and work through any issues that arise in the relationship.

However, meaningful connection doesn't always have to follow a strict plan. Here are a few creative ways to build intimacy and get to know each other on a deeper level:

## Plan Digital Dates

While you may not be able to share a physical space, planning digital dates can make you feel closer. Whether it's watching a movie together using a streaming service with synchronized playback or sharing a meal via video call, these experiences can mimic the feeling of being together in real-time. You can even get creative—take virtual tours of museums, play multiplayer online games, or take a cooking class together through a video tutorial. The goal is to create memories together, even if you're apart.

## Ask Deeper Questions

A great way to foster connection is by asking thoughtful, open-ended questions. Rather than sticking to surface-level topics, dive deeper into life experiences, feelings, and reflections. Plan nights where you take turns asking each other your "favorite" things—favorite book, movie, childhood memory, or even most loved holiday traditions. Then, switch gears and ask about more personal topics, such as the best and worst memories from different points in their life, childhood experiences, family, the scars they carry (both physical and emotional), their health history, and mental health.

Ask about the people who influenced them the most and those who caused them the most pain. These conversations can help you understand your partner's history, values, and how they've become the person they are today. Getting to know someone intimately means going beyond what they do daily and understanding the core of who they are. These questions will help you explore their inner world and build trust and vulnerability between you.

## Set Shared Goals and Create a Bucket List

Even if you're living in different cities or countries, you can still set shared goals and work toward them as a couple. Whether it's learning a new skill together, planning future trips, or saving up for something you both want, having common goals strengthens your bond. You can even create a shared bucket list of experiences you want to have together—places you'd like to visit, activities to try, or milestones to reach in your relationship. This gives you both something to look forward to and reinforces the idea that you're working toward a shared future.

## Host Virtual Game Nights with Friends and Family

To introduce a connection between your partner and your loved ones, consider planning events like a virtual game night where you and your partner each set up a team at your respective locations. This way, your friends and family can get to know your partner and their social circle, and vice versa. You can play trivia games, charades, or other party games that are easy to play over a video call. This not only strengthens your relationship but helps blend your social lives, giving a chance to see how well you fit into each other's worlds. It can sometimes feel as if you are living two different lives and realities which never connect or meet. Making the effort to connect these two parts of your life will have many positive impacts on your relationship.

### Stay Involved in Each Other's Daily Lives

Small, consistent efforts to stay connected throughout the day can have a big impact on your relationship. Simple things like sending a "good morning" text, sharing pictures of what you're doing, or sending a quick voice note can help your partner feel involved in your daily routine. These small gestures create a sense of togetherness even when you're apart. Additionally, sharing little wins, challenges, or even mundane updates from your day can keep the relationship grounded and prevent you from drifting apart.

### Balance Listening and Sharing

When life gets busy, it's easy to fall into the habit of information dumping at the end of a long day. You may feel like you just need to offload everything that happened, but it's important to ensure that your partner gets equal time to share as well. Make a conscious effort to ask questions and truly listen to what they have to say. Balance is key here—both of you should feel heard and understood. Asking follow-up questions, showing empathy, and validating each other's feelings are essential for building emotional closeness. Try to involve your partner by asking them for input and advice on decisions you need to make, whether that is regarding social plans, career decisions or just what to wear to an event, it will help you feel more involved in each other's lives.

## Talk About the Hard Stuff

Getting to know your partner deeply also involves addressing the more challenging or sensitive topics. Don't shy away from talking about mental health, personal struggles, or past traumas. These conversations allow you to be vulnerable with each other, and vulnerability is a powerful way to foster intimacy. Be sure to approach these topics with compassion and respect—ask your partner about their emotional well-being, how they handle stress, and whether they've had to overcome difficult situations in their life. Understanding these aspects of your partner helps you become more attuned to their emotional needs, especially in the context of an LDR, where it may not always be obvious when they're struggling. It may even provide helpful insight which you can use in your own conflicts.

Be sensitive in how you approach these topics, try not to approach as quick fire questions which give a means to an end. Really give each answer time and explore the feelings and long-term effects of what your partner is telling you before moving on.

Connecting on a deeper level in a long-distance relationship requires intentionality, creativity, and the willingness to be vulnerable. By exploring new ways to engage with each other—whether through digital dates, structured activities like those in our recommended book, Close the Distance, or simply sharing your day-to-day life—you can build a strong emotional foundation that withstands the challenges of physical separation. Don't be afraid to dig deeper and ask tough questions. True intimacy goes beyond surface-level interactions and takes time to develop, but the effort you put in will strengthen your bond and make the distance more bearable.

# Chapter 7: Respecting Each Other's Backgrounds and Cultures

One of the most enriching aspects of being in a long-distance relationship (LDR) is the opportunity to connect with someone from a different cultural background. In this chapter, we'll explore the importance of recognizing and appreciating each other's cultures, upbringings, and worldviews, as well as how to navigate potential differences in a way that strengthens your relationship.

Our upbringings shape much of how we see the world, from our core beliefs to how we view family, relationships, gender roles, and even daily routines.

For example, one partner may have grown up in a household with very traditional gender roles, while the other may come from a more egalitarian family where roles were more flexible.

Recognizing and respecting these differences will allow you to navigate potential friction with empathy and understanding. Rather than seeing your differences as barriers, approach them as opportunities to learn and grow together.

### Overcoming Stereotypes and Bias

It's important to avoid falling into the trap of

stereotyping your partner based on their background. Just because someone comes from a certain culture or religious group doesn't mean they will embody all the stereotypes or norms you might associate with that group. Keep an open mind and get to know your partner as an individual rather than assuming things based on generalizations.

Ask questions, be curious, and make the effort to truly understand their personal beliefs and how their upbringing has shaped them.

### Research Your Partner's Heritage

One of the best ways to show respect for your partner's background is to research their heritage and culture. This is especially important if you're planning a visit to their home country or meeting their family, as certain behaviors or comments could unintentionally be offensive.

For instance, some cultures may have specific greetings, customs around gift-giving, or expectations around dress that may differ from your own.

Of course, you should spend plenty of time getting information from the source too! Hearing how these traditions, cultures and social norms influenced your partner's upbringing and who they are today will be both enlightening and connecting for you both.

## Avoid Cultural Misunderstandings

If you're planning to visit your partner's home country, it's a good idea to ask them in advance about cultural norms and expectations so you don't accidentally offend their family or community. This could include learning about acceptable topics of conversation, how to behave during meals, how to dress, norms around make-up, clothing styles or even the shoes you pack or how to address elders.

## Learn Each Other's Language with Duolingo

If you speak different languages, learning your partner's language is another fantastic way to connect on a deeper level. Duolingo is a fun and engaging app that allows you to learn new languages at your own pace. If your partner speaks a language different from your own, why not learn it together? You can make it a fun, shared challenge by comparing weekly scores and helping each other practice.

Not only does learning each other's language show respect, but it also strengthens your communication and deepens your connection by allowing you to understand their world on a more intimate level. It will make your visits more comfortable and show your partner that you are committed to your life together and willing to invest time into your relationship and learning about their world.

Remember it takes a lot of time and commitment to speak fluently so don't get frustrated when you're not learning at the pace you'd like to be. Even being able to speak a few simple words and phrases will be appreciated by their friends and family on your visits.

## Religion and Long-Term Expectations

In many cultures, religion plays a significant role in family life and relationships. If your partner comes from a religious background, it's important to have open discussions about their beliefs and how these might impact your relationship, especially in the long term.

It's crucial to consider how comfortable you are with this possibility and to discuss it openly with your partner. Conversion or adapting to religious practices can be a sensitive and personal decision, so it's important to communicate honestly about your feelings and expectations. Be mindful that converting to a religion is more than just agreeing to be respectful about their beliefs and is a whole lifestyle, often including restrictions around diet, clothing choices, interpersonal relationships and how you handle and approach day to day challenges. It cannot be done half-heartedly and that's very important to recognize.

## Share Your Own Culture

Just as you should take the time to learn about

your partner's background, it's equally important to share your own culture with them. Encourage your partner to ask questions and learn about your traditions and values as well. This mutual exchange can deepen your connection and broaden both of your worldviews. The aim is to learn, share and find your new middle ground, not to simply convert your partner to your view so you don't have to understand theirs.

### Be Open to New Experiences

Cultural differences may sometimes push you out of your comfort zone. Be open to trying new things, whether it's a new food, a different holiday tradition, or a religious practice. These experiences can help you grow both as individuals and as a couple. Being aware of religious holidays and learning enough to send thoughtful seasonal greetings to their family for example can build new layers of love and respect in your relationship.

By taking the time to learn about each other's heritage, asking thoughtful questions, and respecting different values and customs, you can add new dimensions to your relationship and avoid potential misunderstandings.

Remember, you don't have to lose yourself or change your partner to make it work, you're in love with all of your differences and there is no harm in you both staying exactly the same way, it is simply a matter of understanding and embracing the way our culture shapes who we are.

# Chapter 8: Conflict Resolution in Long-Distance Relationships

Conflict is an inevitable part of any relationship, and long-distance relationships (LDRs) are no exception. The challenges of being physically apart can sometimes amplify misunderstandings or feelings of frustration, making effective conflict resolution even more challenging. In this chapter, we'll explore how to approach disagreements in a way that fosters understanding, ensures both partners feel heard, and maintains the health of your relationship, despite the distance.

### Schedule a Time to Talk

When a conflict or disagreement begins within our relationship it can cause a devastating effect on our entire day or even week. Learning how to manage conflicts respectfully can make a huge difference to feelings of security, emotional connection and even our mental health.

One of the simplest ways to remove stress and anxiety around conflict is agreeing not to attempt to resolve conflict whilst you do not have your emotions under control. If you can develop the emotional maturity to recognize when to stop, pause and reflect, you will completely change the way conflict looks.

Top Tips for Conflict Resolution

Believe it or not, there are many factors which can influence the likelihood of a positive resolution. Where possible, you should:

- **Choose the Right Time to Talk** - an ideal time should not be at risk of interruptions and should be when you are both fully engaged and present in the conversation.
- **Address Conflict Via Voice or Video Call Rather Than Text** - texting during conflict can often lead to misinterpretations, as tone and intent can be easily mistaken without essential cues from body language and vocal nuance.
- **Recognize When Emotions Are Too Much** - try to recognize if things start to get heated and suggest the conversation is paused for an emotional reset
- **Set a Timer on the Conversation** – set aside a certain amount of time, whether it is 20, 30 or 60 minutes. If the conflict is not resolved in that time, agree to pause for reflection and pick up again 24 hours later, preventing circular, unhelpful conversation patterns.

Why Resolving Conflicts via Text is Problematic

Texting during a conflict can be problematic for several reasons. Long pauses between responses can also create anxiety or frustration, making it seem like your partner isn't fully engaged in the conversation.

Moreover, texting can often encourage short, blunt responses that don't lend themselves well to resolving emotional issues. It's difficult to express the full range of your feelings through a few sentences, and this can lead to more confusion and hurt feelings. On the other hand, sending long texts in a conflict can come over as an attack on your partner, without allowing them the space to address one point at a time as you would in a conversation. This can lead to one or both of you shutting down. Talking on the phone or on a video call allows for a more fluid, thoughtful discussion, where both partners can clarify things in real-time with emotions and intentions being clearer.

### Choose the Right Time to Call

While voice or video calls are a more constructive space for conflict resolution, it's essential to choose the time carefully. Never rush into a discussion in the heat of the moment when emotions are running high. Take time to cool down, reflect on what's truly bothering you, and gather your thoughts before initiating the conversation. Self-awareness is critical to finding positive and effective solutions in conflict.

You might find it useful to practice some emotional awareness activities first, such as trying to write down why you are upset, what needs or expectations were not met and raised the conflict and what constructive solution you want to come from your discussion. Diving in without a clear picture of these points may create a frustrating circular discussion which remains unresolved. We love **My Book of Big LDR Emotions by Hannah Smart** which has lots of pages for working through LDR based conflicts, insecurities, and anxiety.

### Agree on Ground Rules

Before diving into conflict resolution, it may be helpful to agree to basic ground rules. For example, agree to let each other speak without interruption, avoid blaming language, and agree to pause the conversation if either of you finds they are becoming too emotional or frustrated.

If your disagreement is multifaceted, it may help to agree to work through one topic at a time to ensure you fully work through each aspect and resolve it before moving on.

### Validate Each Other's Feelings

Ensure you are validating each other's feelings. This doesn't mean you have to agree with everything, but it's essential to acknowledge that their emotions are valid. Saying something like, "I understand why you felt upset when that happened," shows empathy, or "I am sorry to hear you felt that way," shows you care about their emotions and how they feel.

## Work Towards Solutions Together

Work together in conflict to find a solution that respects both partners' feelings. This could involve a compromise or even agreeing to see things from a different perspective. The key is to approach the solution as a team, rather than as opponents.

Remember that cultural differences could be at the root of your issues and in that case, you may simply need to agree to be more mindful of each other's beliefs and cultures in future. Being open to different solutions is critical in an LDR. Sometimes, the resolution requires you both to meet in the middle. This might mean adjusting your expectations or finding a creative solution that accommodates both of your needs.

Effective conflict resolution in an LDR requires patience, understanding, and a commitment to listening to each other. By scheduling time to talk, managing your emotions, and respecting each other's perspectives, you can resolve conflicts in a way that strengthens your relationship. Remember, conflict doesn't have to be a negative experience—it can be an opportunity for growth, understanding, and building a deeper connection with your partner.

# Chapter 9: Managing Expectations and Facing Reality

When it comes to long-distance relationships (LDRs), one of the most important things to do early on is to manage expectations. Often, the excitement of love can make couples ignore or downplay some of the significant challenges that lie ahead. While love can be powerful, it's essential to remain practical and realistic about whether your relationship has a viable future. This chapter will help you take a realistic look at the viability of your relationship.

### Be Realistic

Before committing long-term, both partners need to understand their relationship in a broader context. Is your relationship sustainable? Will you be able to close the distance eventually, and if so, when? If not, are you happy spending your lives apart with only brief moments together? These are tough questions, but they are crucial to consider before making any long-term plans.

### Religion, Children, and Commitments

If one or both of you come from a religious background, you should have an open conversation about how this will affect your future together. Is it important for you or your partner to raise your children in a specific place or with a specific religion? Would you be expected to convert? These questions can have a major impact on whether your relationship can survive in the long-term.

Similarly, children from previous relationships play a significant role in the future of your LDR. Moving to another country or city may not be practical if children are involved. For example, if one partner has children who can't be relocated because of custody agreements or schooling, it may limit how much flexibility they have in terms of moving. While this doesn't mean your relationship is doomed, it does mean you'll need to manage expectations around timing and what the future holds. Long-term plans can be made for when children are older, but you must be realistic about how long you're both willing to wait and whether that works for your relationship.

### Pre-Existing Commitments and Responsibilities

Both you and your partner likely have responsibilities that will shape how your future unfolds. This includes skills, qualifications, jobs, family obligations, and personal goals. Have an open and honest conversation about these commitments. If either of you has long-term career ambitions or are deeply connected to your home community, moving may not be feasible. You'll also need to consider whether either of you would be comfortable uprooting your life, and what sacrifices you're willing to make.

For some people, moving away from their support system is non-negotiable. For others, career progression might mean staying in a particular country or city. It's crucial to have these hard conversations early on to prevent future disappointment.

## Travel Restrictions and Legal Barriers

Beyond considering what you are willing to do, you also need to assess what you are able to do. Consider if there are any travel or legal restrictions that could make closing the distance difficult or even impossible. Do either of you have visa restrictions? Are there any financial or legal hurdles in one of your countries that make it hard for a partner to move? If you've never visited each other's countries, it's important to research immigration requirements and residency laws.

Some couples might face restrictions due to health, finances, or even political instability in one partner's country. It's important to acknowledge these potential barriers and evaluate how they may affect your ability to live together permanently. Don't ignore red flags because it's uncomfortable to discuss them; face these realities together.

## Are You Willing to Move?

One of the hardest, but most important, conversations to have is about relocation. Who, if anyone, is willing to move? For a long-distance relationship to have a future, at least one partner will likely need to uproot their life and move to the other's location. If neither of you is willing or able to move, it's essential to acknowledge that early on. It may be that due to restrictions you need to look at both moving to a new country together to make it work, which is a huge leap and expense.

Having this conversation might feel intimidating, but it will prevent heartbreak down the road. Perhaps one partner can relocate after completing their degree or once a work contract ends, or maybe there are factors that can never be compromised. Talk about it directly and be honest about whether relocation is truly possible or if there are immovable obstacles standing in your way.

## Financial Realities

Moving isn't just about emotional readiness—it also requires practical planning, especially around finances. Can you afford to close the distance? Will you both be able to support yourselves financially once one of you relocates? You need to think about the costs of moving, securing housing, and finding employment. Being financially stable as a couple is a key element in ensuring long-term success after closing the distance.

## Long-Term Planning and Hard Conversations

It's essential that couples in long-distance relationships are honest about their long-term future. If you're serious about the relationship, it's necessary to have hard conversations about the logistics of moving, long-term goals, and how to manage commitments. While these discussions may be uncomfortable, they are crucial in avoiding crushing disappointment later on.

Managing expectations and being realistic about the future of your long-distance relationship is a critical step in ensuring long-term success. While it can be difficult to have these tough conversations, they are key to avoiding false hopes or frustration down the road. Both partners must be willing to face reality, ask hard questions, and plan carefully if the goal is to eventually close the distance and share a life together.

Of course, there are many couples who manage the distance long-term and never planned to move, but this is a huge emotional commitment that should not be taken lightly.

# Chapter 10: Celebrating Milestones and Achievements

One of the hardest parts of being in a long-distance relationship is not having your partner by your side for big moments. In this chapter, we'll explore creative ways to acknowledge milestones and achievements and stay connected during significant life events.

### Celebrating Special Occasions from Afar

Special occasions like birthdays, anniversaries, and holidays can feel extra lonely when you're in an LDR. But with a little creativity, you can still make these moments memorable. Virtual celebrations are a great way to make your partner feel loved and appreciated even from a distance. Plan ahead and send thoughtful gifts that arrive on or before the big day. You can also plan a virtual date, like watching a movie together, playing an online game, or cooking the same meal over video chat.

You might also consider synchronized activities, like writing letters to open on the same day or creating a shared playlist of meaningful songs. These small gestures can help maintain a sense of togetherness, even when you're far apart.

## Big Life Events: Weddings, Funerals, and Family Gatherings

It's natural to feel the absence of your partner even more during major life events. Whether it's a joyful occasion like a family wedding or a sad one like a funeral, not having your partner there by your side can feel difficult. However, there are ways to involve your partner, even if they can't attend in person.

A great way to include your partner is to FaceTime or video call them briefly during the event. While it wouldn't be appropriate to stay on a long call during these occasions, a quick chat can make a big difference. For example, at a family wedding, you could give your partner a chance to say hi to everyone and pass on their congratulations. This small moment of connection can help them feel like they're part of the celebration and can show your family that you're committed to keeping your relationship strong, even from afar.

Similarly, during a family birthday party or other special occasion, you can include your partner by sharing a virtual toast or simply having them be present through a brief call to exchange kind words. Maintaining these connections can strengthen your relationship and help your partner feel less excluded from the important moments of your life.

## Personal and Professional Achievements

Celebrating milestones isn't just about birthdays and holidays. Personal and professional achievements, whether it's landing a new job, graduating from school, or reaching a personal goal, are significant moments that could quickly feel isolating and disheartening when you can't have your partner there with you to celebrate.

You might not be there in person to take your partner out for a celebratory dinner, but you can send a thoughtful gift, organize a virtual celebration, or even arrange a surprise delivery of their favorite meal. Be intentional about praising each other's hard work and showing your pride and support for what they've accomplished. If you have some big news due, try to be a little more proactive at checking in and sharing the moment where possible.

## Celebrating Milestones Together

Just because you're far apart doesn't mean you can't celebrate together. One fun way to stay connected is by creating shared goals and working toward them as a couple. For example, you could both set fitness goals, take up a hobby like learning a new language, or work on personal development tasks together. Reaching milestones like these, whether individually or as a team, gives you both something to celebrate, even when you're not physically together.

Another way to celebrate your relationship is by creating a shared bucket list. Write down activities you want to do together in the future, whether that's traveling to a new country, going skydiving, or simply enjoying a weekend getaway. Not only does this give you something to look forward to, but it also helps keep the focus on your long-term commitment to one another.

## Making Each Other Feel Valued

It's important to regularly remind your partner that they are valued, loved, and appreciated. When celebrating big milestones like anniversaries, consider writing a heartfelt letter or sending a video message to express your feelings. While it may seem simple, these small gestures can go a long way in maintaining emotional intimacy.

Beyond the big occasions, find opportunities to celebrate the little things. Did your partner have a hard week at work? Send a supportive text or surprise them with a small gift. Did they finish a challenging project? Plan a virtual toast or watch a movie together to help them unwind. The more you both make an effort to celebrate each other, the more connected you'll feel, even with the physical distance between you.

## Keeping the Connection Strong

In addition to celebrating milestones and achievements, it's essential to keep the connection strong in everyday moments. Make an effort to stay involved in each other's daily lives. Sharing your day-to-day experiences through texts, voice messages, or photos can help you feel more connected and bridge the distance.

You can also motivate each other by sharing your daily to-do lists and checking in on each other's progress. This not only keeps you both productive, but it also fosters a sense of teamwork, even when you're not physically together.

# Chapter 11: Managing the Financial Side of a Long-Distance Relationship

When you're in a long-distance relationship, finances become a significant factor. Travel expenses, maintaining two separate households, and the general cost of living can add up quickly. Without careful planning, money can become a source of stress, but by working together and making smart decisions, you can manage the financial side of your relationship and still prioritize your time together.

## Understanding Financial Realities

The first step to managing finances in a long-distance relationship is being fully aware of each other's financial realities. Currency differences and wage disparities can make a big impact on what each partner is able to contribute. For example, someone living in a country with a lower cost of living may not be able to afford travel or luxuries to the same extent as someone in a wealthier nation.

## Budget-Friendly Travel Strategies

With a bit of planning and careful consideration, you can significantly reduce travel costs. Here are some practical tips:

- Use comparison sites to find the best deals on flights. Websites like Skyscanner, Google Flights, and Kayak are excellent for comparing prices.
- Book two single flights instead of round-trip tickets. Depending on the destination, it may be cheaper for each partner to book their own flight. This is particularly useful if one country has lower taxes or fees on flights.
- Avoid traveling during peak times like school holidays, Christmas, and New Year's. Flights and accommodations are significantly more expensive during these periods. Plan visits during off-peak seasons to take advantage of lower fares.
- Pack light to reduce baggage fees. Traveling with only a carry-on or smaller checked bag can save you money. Consider leaving some essentials at your partner's place to minimize luggage.

### Building a Travel Fund Together

To make your visits more frequent, consider starting a travel fund and challenging yourselves to cut corners in your daily spending. Here are some strategies to help build your travel fund:

- Batch cook and meal prep to save money on groceries. Cooking in bulk reduces waste and avoids expensive takeout. It also cuts down on utility costs.

- Shop sales and buy in bulk. Take advantage of deals and stock up on essentials for significant savings over time.
- Cut out small daily expenses like fancy coffees or lunches out. Invest in a travel mug for coffee from home and bring packed lunches to work.
- Reduce utility bills by cutting heating costs in winter. Wear layers, use blankets, and heat only the rooms you're using to save on energy.
- Use automatic roundups on your bank account. This feature rounds up your transactions to the nearest whole amount and deposits the change into savings.

### Cutting Costs at Home

While travel is a major expense, everyday living costs also impact your budget. Consider these adjustments to save more:

- Get a roommate if you live alone. Sharing rent and utilities can significantly reduce your expenses.
- Work extra shifts or a part-time job. Additional work can help save for visits, making the effort worthwhile knowing it supports your relationship.
- Save on transportation by using public transit, carpooling, or biking. Consider a more economical or cheaper-to-insure car.

## Financial Planning for the Long Term

Managing finances in an LDR isn't just about budgeting for the next visit—it's also about long-term planning. If your relationship becomes more serious, you'll need to discuss plans to close the distance and potentially move in together. This transition requires careful financial planning, including:

- Considering where you'll live and whether one partner will need to change jobs.
- Evaluating work restrictions that may impact relocation. If one partner has a job that doesn't offer remote work or if other commitments make moving difficult, factor these into your planning.
- Assessing visa or immigration costs. These can be expensive, so be fully aware of the costs and legal steps involved.

## Encouraging Each Other to Stay on Track

Support each other in your financial goals. Share progress, celebrate milestones (like reaching savings goals), and hold each other accountable without being controlling. Make saving fun rather than punitive.

Motivate each other with challenges, like seeing who can save the most in a month or cut out unnecessary expenses. Keeping each other engaged will make the financial sacrifices feel like a team effort.

Managing the financial side of a long-distance relationship may seem overwhelming, but with careful planning and teamwork, it's entirely possible to make it work.

Most importantly, support each other's efforts, knowing that every bit saved brings you closer to the next visit and building a future together.

# Chapter 12: Planning for the Future

In long-distance relationships (LDRs), future planning can be one of the most challenging yet essential conversations. It's exciting to think about closing the distance, moving in together, or even getting married, but these discussions also come with a great deal of emotional and practical pressure. That's why it's important to approach them realistically, with patience, and to avoid rushing into any major life decisions.

### Breaking Down Future Plans

It's easy to feel overwhelmed when you start thinking about the future. Questions like "Where will we live?", "Who will move?", and "How will we afford it?" can weigh heavily on your mind. That's where having structured conversations becomes helpful. Instead of tackling everything at once, break future planning into manageable pieces.

By taking the time to break down your future into smaller, bite-sized conversations, you'll reduce the stress that often comes with these topics and feel more prepared to tackle them as a team.

### Be Realistic and Patient

As exciting as it may be to plan for your future together, it's crucial to remain realistic. Long-distance relationships require time and patience, especially when it comes to making life-changing decisions like moving, marriage, or merging your lives. Don't rush into marriage or make decisions based on the pressure of being apart. Instead, make sure you're both on the same page about what you want for your future.

It's important to understand each other's circumstances before making any decisions. It also helps if you are both realistic about the fact that life changes our plans often, so you may end up on a completely different path to the one you agreed in the beginning.

### Avoid Rushing Into Major Decisions

It's tempting to want to close the distance as quickly as possible, especially if you've been apart for a long time. However, rushing into major life decisions like moving in together or getting married can put unnecessary strain on the relationship. Take the time to get to know each other's day-to-day lives, make sure your goals align, and have realistic expectations for how your lives will merge.

Remember that the transition from a long-distance relationship to living together will bring its own set of challenges. It's easy to idealize the relationship when you're apart, but day-to-day realities—like managing finances, balancing personal space, and navigating each other's routines—can be much harder than you imagined. Taking your time to get there will make that transition smoother and give you both more confidence in your decisions. It is also helpful if you can have some prolonged visits before the big move of up to a month or more, so you can see how you work together when you're not in holiday mode.

### Make Future Planning Fun and Engaging

Planning for the future doesn't have to be daunting. Make it enjoyable by incorporating activities that help you discuss your future in a positive, engaging way. For example, you and your partner could:

- Create a shared bucket list of experiences and goals you both want to achieve.
- Set short-term and long-term goals for your relationship, whether it's seeing each other more frequently, saving for a big move, or discussing where you'd like to settle.
- Create a shared vision board

By making these discussions enjoyable and goal-oriented, you can take some of the pressure off and approach your future planning with optimism.

### Communicating About Expectations and Goals

It's essential to communicate openly about your expectations for the future. What does closing the distance look like for both of you? Where do you see yourselves living? How will you navigate work, family commitments, and finances once you're together? These are big questions that need honest and clear communication.

It's also important to discuss any potential cultural differences or long-term expectations regarding family roles, gender roles, or religious beliefs. These can have a big impact on future plans, so being open and respectful about your needs and expectations will help you both understand whether your long-term goals align.

# Chapter 13: Navigating Social Media in a Long-Distance Relationship

Social media plays an important role in relationships today, especially in long-distance relationships (LDRs). It can help you feel connected, but it can also create complications that can strain your relationship if not handled carefully. Jealousy, misunderstandings, and a lack of clarity around boundaries can make social media a constant source of stress and upset.

### Jealousy, Insecurities, and Online Presence

Social media can amplify insecurities, especially when you're in a long-distance relationship. Without being physically present, it's easy for your partner to feel left out, jealous, or insecure about what you're doing and who you're spending time with.

To manage this, you and your partner should try not to surprise each other with social media posts. If you're going out with friends, let your partner know beforehand so that they hear it directly from you, rather than seeing it unexpectedly in a post or story. This way, they won't be blindsided or make assumptions about your plans or company.

Without regular in-person interaction, it's easy for insecurities to arise. Misunderstandings or assumptions about what's happening in a photo or who you're with can lead to unnecessary conflict. By keeping your partner informed in real-time, you ensure that they remain a part of your life—even when you're far apart—and you help prevent any negative feelings from building up. Being proactive can also show that you value their presence in your life, even if it's from a distance. If talking during would interrupt the flow of your plans, make the effort to reach out before and after so your partner knows they are on your mind and that you are home safe.

**Setting Boundaries for Social Media Sharing**

When you're in an LDR, it's important to set clear boundaries on what you both are comfortable sharing about your relationship online. Some people are private and prefer to keep their personal lives off social media, while others enjoy sharing more. It's crucial to talk about this early on to avoid any missteps.

For example, you might be okay with posting pictures of each other or announcing your relationship status, but your partner may want to wait until they've informed family or their children. It's essential to respect each other's comfort levels and agree on how much to share about your relationship. Misunderstandings can happen if one partner shares too much too soon or in a way that the other isn't comfortable with.

Keep in mind that these boundaries can change

over time. As your relationship progresses and you both grow more comfortable, you might want to share more publicly. Just remember to check in with each other periodically to ensure you're both still on the same page about what to post and what to keep private.

If your partner is from a different culture, it's worth taking the time to learn more about their social norms around online presence, as it could help you avoid misunderstandings. This respect for each other's comfort zones, boundaries, and cultural practices can foster greater trust in the relationship.

## Managing Public Perception of Your Relationship

In addition to setting boundaries around what you share about your relationship, it's also important to manage how much of your relationship is open to public scrutiny. Some couples love sharing cute moments, tagging each other, or commenting on each other's posts. Others prefer a more private approach.

When in a long-distance relationship, public interactions can become the main form of connection that your family and friends see, so it's natural to feel pressure to keep up appearances. However, be mindful not to post things that put pressure on your relationship or make it appear differently from reality. Overemphasizing how perfect things are online can create unrealistic expectations, both for you and for others watching your relationship unfold.

On the other hand, if you or your partner prefer to keep things quiet, make sure you both agree on what's best for your relationship. And if your social circle knows about your relationship, ensure your posts don't fuel assumptions or rumors.

## Navigating the Impact of Social Media on Mental Health

While social media is a convenient tool for staying connected, it can also have negative impacts on mental health if not managed properly. Constantly checking on each other's social media profiles or seeing your partner interacting with other people can lead to overthinking, stress, and unwarranted jealousy.

If you find that social media is causing tension or mental strain, take a step back and discuss how it affects both of you. Be honest about what triggers insecurities or anxiety, and work together to find solutions. This might involve spending less time on social media or creating some space between each other's online activity to maintain your emotional well-being.

Sometimes, it might be necessary to take social media breaks to focus more on direct communication and less on public interaction. Discuss if this might benefit your relationship and ensure it's mutual.

## Avoiding Misunderstandings and Assumptions

Social media posts are often snapshots of a moment in time, and they rarely show the full story. As such, it's easy to misinterpret a post, comment, or tag, especially when you're in a long-distance relationship. If something on your partner's social media profile doesn't sit well with you, talk to them about it directly rather than making assumptions. Miscommunication is one of the biggest sources of conflict in LDRs, and social media can make that worse if not handled properly.

A simple conversation can clear up misunderstandings, while jumping to conclusions can lead to unnecessary conflicts. Be open and honest with each other, and always seek clarity rather than harboring doubts.

In conclusion, social media in an LDR can be both a gift and a challenge. By communicating openly, respecting each other's boundaries, and managing expectations, it can serve as a bridge that keeps you and your partner connected. However, if left unchecked, it can also introduce unnecessary tension. Be mindful, patient, and always prioritize your relationship over the need to portray perfection online.

# Chapter 14: Patience and Perseverance

In a long-distance relationship (LDR), the virtue of patience becomes one of your greatest assets. Navigating the emotional ups and downs while being physically separated from your partner can often be challenging but learning to cultivate patience and perseverance can be the key to staying connected and growing stronger together.

### The Power of Patience

One of the hardest parts of an LDR is the waiting game—whether it's waiting for the next visit, waiting for a message, or simply waiting for the day when you can finally close the distance. These periods of waiting can feel endless, and it's easy to get frustrated, anxious, or feel disconnected. However, learning to embrace patience during these times can shift your mindset and help maintain harmony in the relationship.

### Patience in an LDR means:

- Trusting your partner, even when communication is less frequent or delayed.
- Understanding that life happens, and sometimes work, time zones, or personal responsibilities may prevent them from

being as available as you'd like.
- Realizing that not every visit or conversation will be perfect. There will be ups and downs, but remaining patient with each other helps you weather these fluctuations together.

Remember, patience isn't about passively waiting—it's about actively accepting the situation for what it is while working towards a better future together.

**Perseverance Through Challenges**

Perseverance is another critical quality in an LDR. There will be moments when the distance feels overwhelming or when conflicts arise due to miscommunication or unmet expectations. These are the times when both partners need to remind themselves why they're in the relationship and be willing to work through the rough patches together.

Perseverance involves:

- Pushing through tough moments when the loneliness becomes hard to bear or when external circumstances make it difficult to connect.
- Believing in the long-term vision of your relationship. When you're committed to a future together, the obstacles of today feel more manageable.
- Working on solutions together—whether

that's planning future visits, figuring out financial constraints, or simply talking through issues, it's important to keep the conversation going, even when things seem difficult.

It's helpful to recognize that relationships—whether long-distance or not—require effort and persistence. There will be challenges but enduring them and finding ways to overcome them together will strengthen the bond you share.

### Handling Setbacks with Grace

No matter how well you plan, setbacks will happen in a long-distance relationship. Maybe your partner has to cancel a visit, or perhaps an unexpected financial burden keeps you apart longer than anticipated. These moments can feel crushing, but the key is to handle setbacks with grace and understanding.

When setbacks occur:

- Communicate openly with your partner. Share your feelings but also be understanding of the situation.
- Shift your focus from the setback to how you'll work through it together. Whether that's scheduling a new visit or finding alternative ways to stay connected, focus on what you can control.
- Remain flexible. Being rigid in expectations can create unnecessary stress. While

planning is important, it's equally important to remain open to changes and adapt to new circumstances.

Long-distance relationships demand flexibility and resilience. By approaching challenges with a solution-focused mindset, you can avoid allowing setbacks to damage the connection you've built.

### Cultivating Emotional Resilience

Another important aspect of perseverance in an LDR is emotional resilience—the ability to bounce back from emotional lows and maintain a positive outlook. When you're apart, it's easy for negative emotions like loneliness, frustration, or insecurity to take over. But developing emotional resilience can help you regain balance and keep the relationship strong.

Here's how to build emotional resilience in an LDR:

- Take care of yourself emotionally and mentally. Prioritize self-care and mental health so that you're in the best place to support yourself and your partner.
- Stay connected with your support system. Make sure you have friends, family, or a therapist to talk to about your feelings. They can offer perspective and help you process any emotional struggles.
- Find constructive ways to cope. Journaling, meditating, exercising, or engaging in

hobbies are all healthy outlets for emotional stress. When you manage your own well-being, you're less likely to let negative emotions spill over into your relationship.

Building emotional resilience ensures that both you and your partner can navigate the emotional rollercoaster of a long-distance relationship without letting it derail your progress.

## Celebrating Progress

Lastly, it's important to celebrate your progress as a couple. LDRs are difficult, and every milestone you reach together—whether it's a successful visit, resolving a conflict, or simply getting through a tough week—is worth celebrating. By acknowledging and appreciating these small victories, you remind yourselves of the strength and commitment you both bring to the relationship.

Whether it's setting a date for your next visit, overcoming a challenge together, or just staying connected in a meaningful way, take the time to reflect on how far you've come. Patience and perseverance aren't easy, but they're rewarded when you see how your bond deepens through the challenges you've faced together.

In summary, long-distance relationships require a combination of patience, perseverance, and emotional resilience. The distance will test you, but with a clear understanding of what you're working toward, the ability to manage setbacks, and realistic expectations, you can build a relationship that thrives despite the miles between you. By staying focused on the long-term goal and continually investing in the relationship, you and your partner can weather the challenges of distance and emerge even stronger together.

# Chapter 15: Creating Intimacy and Anticipation Without Physical Closeness

Maintaining a sense of intimacy when you can't be physically close can be tough. While physical intimacy is important in most relationships, long-distance couples need to find creative ways to keep the connection alive and create a sense of anticipation without being in the same room. Intimacy isn't just about physical closeness—it's about emotional bonding, vulnerability, and shared experiences.

### The Importance of Flirting and Complimenting Each Other

Flirting is a fun and playful way to keep the spark alive in an LDR. Just because you're miles apart doesn't mean the playful banter, teasing, and excitement that comes from flirting has to disappear. Flirt with each other over text, voice messages, or video calls—sending a quick "thinking of you" or playful tease can instantly create a moment of connection and excitement.

Equally important is complimenting each other. Verbal affirmations and positive reinforcement go a long way in helping both partners feel desired, appreciated, and confident. Take time to compliment each other, whether it's about physical appearance, something they've achieved, or simply the way they make you feel. Compliments are small gestures that can foster emotional intimacy even in the absence of physical closeness.

## Creative Ways to Keep the Fire Going

While physical touch may be off the table, there are many ways to maintain intimacy and build anticipation in your relationship from a distance. Here are a few ideas:

- Send thoughtful gifts: Surprise your partner with a gift that shows you're thinking of them—something meaningful or connected to an inside joke can create a sense of closeness.
- Plan date nights: Have regular digital dates where you cook and eat dinner together over video, watch a movie simultaneously, or play a game. The effort you put into these moments helps to recreate the shared experiences you'd have if you were together.
- Share your day-to-day life: Send photos or voice notes of the little things in your life— what you're cooking, the view from your walk, a new book you're reading. This keeps your partner involved in the small moments and helps create a sense of being

"together."
- Build anticipation for future visits: Talk about what you'll do the next time you're together, from shared experiences to intimate moments. Building excitement for the next visit helps you both look forward to something tangible.

## Boundaries Around Intimacy

When it comes to more intimate aspects of a relationship, it's important to establish clear boundaries and ensure that both partners feel comfortable. In an LDR, you may be tempted to explore intimacy through text messages, photos, or video, but it's crucial to prioritize consent and mutual comfort at every step.

- Consent is key: Intimate texts, photos, or videos should never be sent without clear and explicit consent. Just as in a physical relationship, both partners need to be comfortable with the level of intimacy being shared. If you're unsure, ask your partner what they're comfortable with.
- Respect each other's boundaries: If your partner sets a boundary, it's essential to respect it. This could mean refraining from sending certain kinds of messages or respecting their privacy when they need space. Crossing a boundary can lead to feelings of discomfort, mistrust, or even resentment, so open communication is

critical.

## What to Do If a Boundary Is Crossed

If your partner crosses a boundary, whether intentional or not, it's important to address the issue right away. Here's what you can do if that happens:

- Communicate clearly: Tell your partner how their actions made you feel and why it's important for them to respect your boundary. Use "I" statements to express your feelings without placing blame.
- Reestablish your boundary: Make sure your partner understands where your boundary lies and why it matters. Boundaries are about mutual respect, and it's okay to reaffirm them when necessary.
- Assess their response: A healthy response from your partner should involve respect, understanding, and a willingness to adjust their behavior. If your partner disregards your boundaries or pressures you, that's a red flag and should be addressed seriously.

## The Dangers of Sending Intimate Photos

In the digital age, many couples experiment with sending intimate photos or videos. While this can be a fun way to maintain intimacy, it also comes with risks. Once something is sent digitally, it's out of your control and could potentially be shared, even if your partner has no malicious intent.

Here are a few guidelines to protect yourself:

- Think before you send: Before sharing any intimate content, ask yourself if you're comfortable with the possibility of it being seen by others. Even in a trusting relationship, accidents happen—phones get stolen, or messages get sent to the wrong person.
- Avoid showing identifiable features: If you do choose to send intimate photos, consider ways to protect your identity. Avoid showing your face, tattoos, or other identifying marks to reduce the risk of it being linked back to you.
- Use secure apps: If you do share intimate content, consider using secure messaging apps with encryption and disappearing messages. This can add an extra layer of protection, though it's not foolproof.

### Creative Ways to Stay Intimate Without Risk

If you want to maintain intimacy without the risk of sending explicit photos or texts, there are plenty of creative alternatives:

- Send teasing photos: Instead of sending intimate images, share playful or flirty photos—maybe it's just your legs under a blanket, a close-up of a smile, or a picture

of you in a favorite outfit. It can be suggestive without being explicit.
- Write intimate letters: Writing a heartfelt letter or sending a voice note can be just as intimate as sharing photos. Pour your feelings into words, share your fantasies, or reflect on moments you've shared together.
- Plan intimate conversations: Set aside time for intimate or deep conversations where you share your desires, talk about your future together, or reminisce about moments you've had in person. Emotional intimacy can often be more powerful than physical.

Maintaining intimacy in a long-distance relationship requires creativity, communication, and mutual respect. By flirting, complimenting, and sharing moments from your lives, you can keep the emotional connection strong. Establishing clear boundaries around intimacy and respecting them is essential for trust and comfort. Always prioritize consent, and if you choose to explore physical intimacy digitally, be mindful of the risks and find ways to protect yourselves.

Intimacy isn't just about the physical—it's about the emotional connection that grows from sharing, understanding, and being vulnerable with each other. With a little creativity, you can keep the fire alive, even when miles apart.

# Chapter 16: Coping with Time Zones and Schedules

One of the unique and often frustrating aspects of long-distance relationships (LDRs) is managing time zones and schedules. It's challenging enough to balance two busy lives when you're in the same place, but when you add in time differences, it can feel like you're constantly missing each other or struggling to find time to connect. However, with some planning, patience, and creativity, you can bridge the time gap and keep your relationship strong.

### Managing Different Time Zones

If you and your partner live in different time zones, you'll quickly realize that coordinating your schedules requires extra effort. When one of you is waking up, the other may be winding down for the day. The key is time zone management: finding moments when your schedules overlap and making the most of those windows of opportunity.

- Use time zone apps: Apps like Time Zone Buddy or World Clock make it easier to track time differences and find ideal times for both of you to connect. Once you've figured out a general rhythm, you can build a routine around it.

- Set expectations: Be realistic about when you'll be able to communicate. You may not be able to talk every morning or evening, but you can make the most of the time you have.
- Creative solutions: Hannah Smart's book Close the Distance offers great tasks designed to help couples overcome time zone challenges. It includes fun and engaging activities that can be done asynchronously, helping you feel connected even if you're not available at the same time.

**Scheduling Calls and Video Chats**

If you're navigating your relationship around different time zones, you may find pre-planning your call times works best, but it's also important to stay flexible. Here's how to approach it:

- Create a daily routine: Establish a time that works for both of you to catch up, whether it's in the morning, during lunch, or late at night. If one of you is more of a morning person and the other is a night owl, you can plan to connect at those times.
- Be flexible: While routines are helpful, be open to the fact that some days, catching up just won't be possible. On those days, try sending little updates—photos, voice notes, or messages throughout the day—so that when you do catch up, you haven't

missed everything.
- Honor your commitments: If you've scheduled a call, try to stick to it. Cancelling frequently or showing up late can build resentment or make your partner feel less important. Consistency helps build trust and reliability.

**Balancing Scheduling and Spontaneity**

While scheduling is necessary in a long-distance relationship, spontaneity is equally important. Too much structure can take the magic out of things. Mixing in a little surprise can keep your relationship feeling fresh and exciting.

- Send spontaneous notes or selfies: When you're thinking about your partner, send them a quick "thinking of you" message, a voice note, or a selfie. This small act can go a long way in making your partner feel cherished, even if you can't have a full conversation.
- Leave video or voice messages: If your partner is asleep or busy, leave them a message they can wake up to or listen to during a break. This keeps the connection alive, even when you're operating on different schedules.

**Coping with Fatigue and Frustration**

When you're dealing with time zone differences

and mismatched schedules, fatigue and frustration are inevitable. Some days, you may feel like you're constantly missing each other, and it's easy for that frustration to build up. Here are a few ways to manage it:

- Be patient with each other: Time zones and scheduling issues are no one's fault. Practice empathy and try to understand when your partner can't talk because of their obligations or time constraints. A little understanding goes a long way in reducing frustration.
- Communicate your needs: If you're feeling disconnected, let your partner know. It's better to have an honest conversation about your feelings than to let frustration simmer. They might not realize how much you miss talking, and together you can brainstorm solutions.
- Manage your expectations: Don't compare your LDR to conventional relationships where couples can see each other daily. Your relationship is unique, and the challenges you face are part of that. Focus on what you can control and take pride in the fact that you're making the effort to stay connected despite the distance.

### Planning for the Future

Finally, when time zones and schedules become difficult, it helps to remember that this situation is (hopefully) temporary. Having a long-term plan to close the distance can provide hope and a light at the end of the tunnel. Even if that plan is far off, knowing there's a timeline in place can help you both stay patient and focused.

# Chapter 17: Maintaining Independence in LDRs

In any relationship, it's important to maintain a sense of self, but in a long-distance relationship (LDR), it becomes even more crucial. With physical distance between you, it can be easy to overcompensate by becoming emotionally or mentally dependent on your partner. However, striking the right balance between togetherness and autonomy is key to maintaining a healthy relationship—and ensuring your own personal growth along the way.

### Maintaining Your Sense of Self

When you're in an LDR, the time spent talking to your partner often becomes the highlight of your day, but you still need to focus on your own hobbies, friends, and interests. Maintaining your sense of self helps you stay grounded and fulfilled as an individual, which in turn strengthens your relationship.

- Whether it's a hobby, a new skill, or a passion project, having something that's yours can help you stay focused and give you a sense of accomplishment outside of the relationship.
- Stay connected with your support network: Your friends and family play a vital role in

your life. Make time for them, share what's happening in your life, and avoid isolating yourself because you're too wrapped up in your relationship.
- Practice self-care: Your emotional and mental well-being should always be a priority. Make sure you're setting aside time to relax, recharge, and care for yourself, so you're in the best headspace when you connect with your partner.

**Avoiding Co-dependency**

Long-distance relationships can sometimes foster emotional dependency or even codependency, where one or both partners become overly reliant on each other for emotional support, validation, or happiness. While it's natural to seek comfort and reassurance from your partner, it's essential that you both maintain your independence.

- Set healthy boundaries: Establish clear boundaries for how much time you'll spend talking to each other and when you'll focus on other aspects of your life. This can help prevent feelings of suffocation or over-reliance.
- Limit constant communication: It's tempting to want to be in touch all day long, but over-communication can lead to dependency. Give each other space to live your own lives and come back together to share experiences. This makes your

conversations more meaningful and allows both of you to grow individually.
- Don't expect your partner to fulfill all your emotional needs: It's important to have other outlets for emotional support, such as close friends or family. This reduces the pressure on your partner and ensures you're not placing too much emotional weight on them.

### Pursuing Personal Goals

One of the strengths of an LDR is the opportunity for both partners to pursue their personal goals without distractions. Use the distance as a way to focus on self-improvement and growth, whether it's advancing in your career, furthering your education, or mastering a new skill. While supporting each other's ambitions is essential, make sure you're also celebrating your own accomplishments.

A strong relationship is built on mutual support. Encourage your partner to follow their passions and achieve their personal milestones and be each other's biggest cheerleader through the process. Remember these individual wins and progressive moves will no doubt support your life together eventually.

Maintaining independence in an LDR is about finding the balance between staying connected with your partner and nurturing your own sense of self. By avoiding codependency, pursuing personal goals, and respecting each other's need for autonomy, you create a strong foundation for a healthy relationship. Growth doesn't stop just because you're apart, if anything, the distance gives you the opportunity to become even stronger as individuals and as a couple.

# Chapter 18: When to Walk Away

Long-distance relationships can be incredibly rewarding, but they can also present unique challenges that make it difficult to maintain a healthy connection. While some obstacles can be overcome with time, effort, and communication, there may come a point when continuing the relationship no longer serves either partner. In this chapter, we'll explore how to recognize when an LDR may not be working, when to consider walking away, and how to navigate the emotional process of ending things respectfully.

## Recognizing the Signs That an LDR May No Longer Be Working

It can be tough to admit when a relationship isn't going well, but recognizing the signs that it may no longer be working is essential for both your emotional well-being and the health of the partnership. Here are some warning signs to look out for:

- **Consistent lack of communication:** If you or your partner are no longer putting in the effort to connect regularly or find it exhausting to maintain the relationship, it could be a sign that the emotional connection is fading.
- **Feeling unfulfilled or disconnected:** Over

time, if you notice that you feel more lonely in the relationship than supported, or if the emotional connection isn't enough to sustain you anymore, it might be time to reconsider your relationship.
- **Constant arguing:** Disagreements and conflicts are natural, but if you and your partner can't seem to get through conversations without tension, resentment, or unresolved issues, it may indicate deeper problems that can't be easily fixed.
- **Growing resentment:** If either of you begins to feel resentment for making sacrifices for the relationship or for unmet needs, it's important to address those feelings before they fester.
- **Not envisioning a future together:** If the idea of closing the distance seems more and more impossible or undesirable, and neither partner can realistically commit to a future together, it may be a sign that the relationship has run its course.

Discussing Dealbreakers and When to Consider Ending a Long-Distance Relationship

Every relationship has its dealbreakers, and it's important to be honest with yourself and your partner about what those are. When it comes to long-distance relationships, some common dealbreakers might include:

- **Trust issues or infidelity:** Trust is a

cornerstone of any relationship, but in an LDR, it becomes even more critical. If trust is broken or one partner feels insecure, it's essential to address it openly. Without trust, the relationship may become unsustainable.
- **Incompatible long-term goals:** If one partner wants children and the other doesn't, or if neither of you is willing or able to relocate in the future, these are major incompatibilities that can be difficult to overcome.
- **Emotional neglect:** If one or both of you are no longer emotionally invested in the relationship, and attempts to reconnect aren't working, it may be time to consider ending things.
- **Cultural, religious, or lifestyle differences:** Sometimes, deep-seated differences in values, religion, or culture can become dealbreakers if they prevent you from seeing eye-to-eye on major life decisions.

When these or other dealbreakers arise, it's important to have honest conversations about the future and whether continuing the relationship is in both of your best interests.

### Understanding the Difference Between Temporary Challenges and Fundamental Incompatibilities

Every long-distance relationship will face

challenges, and it's crucial to distinguish between temporary hurdles and fundamental incompatibilities.

## Temporary Challenges

These might include issues like a stressful job, financial struggles, or a short-term communication breakdown. While difficult, these challenges can often be worked through with time and effort. Ask yourself: Is this something we can overcome together with better communication, patience, or compromise?

## Fundamental Incompatibilities

On the other hand, some issues—like different life goals, core values, or a lack of emotional connection—are often impossible to resolve. In these cases, it's essential to acknowledge when the relationship isn't working and move on before more hurt is caused.

## Consider Space Instead

Sometimes, the challenges posed by an LDR just need a little time to process and work through. Be open to giving yourselves a little space from each other to see if something you thought was a fundamental incompatibility may in fact be a temporary challenge with time and perspective.

## How to Break Up Respectfully

Ending any relationship is difficult, but ending a long-distance relationship comes with its own unique challenges. It's essential to break up in a way that is respectful to both partners and allows for closure.

- **Choose the right time and method:** If possible, try to have the breakup conversation over video call or phone rather than text. This allows for more meaningful communication and respect for each other's emotions.
- **Be honest but kind:** Explain your reasons for ending the relationship clearly and honestly but avoid unnecessary hurt. Focus on how you feel rather than placing blame on your partner.
- **Give each other space:** After the breakup, it's important to allow both yourself and your partner time to heal. Limit contact for a while to help both of you move on.
- **Acknowledge the good:** Even if the relationship didn't work out, acknowledge the positive aspects of your time together and what you've learned from the experience.

## Moving On and Healing After Ending a Long-Distance Relationship

Once the relationship ends, it's natural to feel

sadness, loss, or even relief. Healing takes time, but there are ways to help yourself move forward:

- **Lean on your support network:** Talk to friends or family about how you're feeling, and don't be afraid to seek professional help if needed.
- **Give yourself time to grieve:** It's okay to feel sad, angry, or heartbroken. Allow yourself the emotional space to process the breakup.
- **Focus on self-care:** Take time to do things that bring you joy, whether it's hobbies, exercise, or spending time with loved ones. Prioritize your emotional well-being.
- **Learn from the experience:** Every relationship teaches us something, even if it doesn't last forever. Reflect on what you've learned and how it can help you grow in future relationships.

Walking away from a long-distance relationship is never easy but recognizing when it's the right decision is an important part of protecting your emotional health and well-being. By understanding the difference between temporary challenges and deal breaking incompatibilities, you can make an informed decision about when it's time to let go. And while the breakup process is painful, giving yourself time to heal and reflect can help you emerge stronger, wiser, and ready for whatever comes next.

# Books for Long-Distance Couples:

### "Close the Distance" by Hannah Smart

This book provides weekly challenges and activities for long-distance couples to deepen their connection and grow closer, offering 52 weekly tasks designed to tackle all aspects of a relationship.

### "The 5 Love Languages: The Secret to Love That Lasts" by Gary Chapman

Understanding each other's love languages is crucial in any relationship, especially in LDRs where physical touch and quality time might be limited. This book can help you and your partner discover new ways to show love even from afar.

### "Attached: The New Science of Adult Attachment and How It Can Help You Find—and Keep—Love" by Amir Levine and Rachel Heller

This book focuses on attachment styles and understanding how you and your partner may relate to each other emotionally, which is especially useful when navigating an LDR.

### "Love in the Time of Distance: How to Maintain a Successful Long-Distance Relationship" by Claire Kelley

A helpful guide packed with tips, stories, and strategies specifically for long-distance couples, addressing common concerns like trust, communication, and intimacy.

### "The Long-Distance Relationship Survival Guide: Secrets and Strategies from Successful Couples Who Have Gone the Distance" by Chris Bell and Kate Brauer-Bell

Written by a couple who survived a long-distance relationship, this book offers practical advice, communication tips, and examples of how to overcome LDR challenges.

# Links for Long-Distance Couples:

### 16 Personalities

For the Meyers-Brigg Test

https://www.16personalities.com

### Love Language Quiz

To discover your love language

https://5lovelanguages.com

### Attachment Style Quiz

To discover and compare your attachment style

https://attachment.personaldevelopmentschool.com

Printed in Great Britain
by Amazon